This book belongs to:

Design and Technology in Today's World: A First Look

with Professor Baz

Years 3–6

Published by
Professor Baz

Design and Technology in Today's World: A First Look
Basil Slynko

Editor: Sandra Balonyi
Text designer: Michael Haddad
Cover designer: Michael Haddad
Cover image: Paul Lennon and Shutterstock
Illustrator: Paul Lennon

First published in Australia in 2018
Copyright ©2018 Basil Slynko

Copyright Notice
This Work is copyright. No part of this Work may be reproduced, stored in a retrieval system, or transmitted in any form or by any means without prior written permission of the publisher. Except as permitted under the Copyright Act 1968, for example any fair dealing for the purposes of private study, research, criticism or review, subject to certain limitations. These limitations include: restricting the copying to a maximum of one chapter or 10% of this book, whichever is greater; providing an appropriate notice and warning with the copies of the Work disseminated; taking all reasonable steps to limit access to these copies to people authorised to receive these copies; ensuring you hold the appropriate Licences issued by the Copyright Agency Limited ("CAL"), supply a remuneration notice to CAL and pay any required fees. For details of CAL licences and remuneration notices please contact CAL at Level 11, 266 Goulburn Street, Sydney NSW 2000.
Tel: (02) 9394 7600, Fax: (02) 9394 7601
Email: info@copyright.com.au
Website: www.copyright.com.au

For permission to use material from this text, please contact the publisher.
Email: **info@professorbaz.com.au**

National Library of Australia Cataloguing-in-Publication Data

Slynko, Basil.
Design and Technology in Today's World: A First Look

ISBN: 978-0-6484052-0-7
For primary school age.

Printed in Australia
2 3 4 5 6 7 8 9 10 27 26 25 24 23 22 21 20

Contents

Acknowledgements iv

Introduction v
To the Teacher vi
To the Student ix
KWL Chart x

Units
1. What is technology? 2
2. What is design? 4
3. Materials 8
4. Tools 11
5. Processes 14
6. What is a system? 16
   - 6A – Technological systems 17
   - 6B – Agricultural systems 19
   - 6C – Control systems 20
7. Technology and the future 21
8. Safety 23

Find-a-word 24

Activity Sheets
1. What is technology? 26
2. What is design? 28
3. Materials 30
4. Tools 32
5. Processes 34
6. What is a system? 36
   - 6A – 1 Technological systems: Manufacturing 37
   - 6A – 2 Technological systems: Construction 39
   - 6B – Agricultural systems 41
   - 6C – Control systems 43
7. Technology and the future 44
8. Safety 49

Acknowledgements

The author and publisher would like to credit or acknowledge the following sources for permission to use copyright material:
Fotolia: p. 26 (right); Makita (Australia) Pty Ltd: pp. 11, 13; E Shambrook p. 11 (universal equipment, bottom); Queensland Rail: p. 23 (top); Seton Australia Pty Ltd: pp. 44, 49; Shutterstock: pp. v, ix, 11 (industrial equipment), 17 (bottom), 19, 21, 22, 26 (left); Stanley Black & Decker, Inc: p. 13 (bottom right).

Every attempt has been made to trace and acknowledge copyright holders. Where attempts have been unsuccessful, the publisher welcomes information that would redress the situation.

The author and publisher wish to thank the following individuals for the helpful advice they gave during the writing of this book: Julia Horn, Esther Pratt, Jonathan Francis, Melissa Slynko and Bob Hibbard (Agricultural systems).

The author and publisher also wish to thank the following individuals for their assistance: David Millward, Queensland Rail; Lindsay Hart, Mitre 10 Mega, Beenleigh; and the staff at Trade Tools, Burleigh.

A big thank you to these wonderful students: Alex B, Jesse B, Sarah B, Charlotte M, Rebekah P and Tameika P, who reviewed the text and completed the Activity Sheets. Their feedback was invaluable.

A special 'thank you!' to Paul Lennon, Michael Haddad and Sandra Balonyi for working with me on this project.

Responsibility for errors remains with the author.

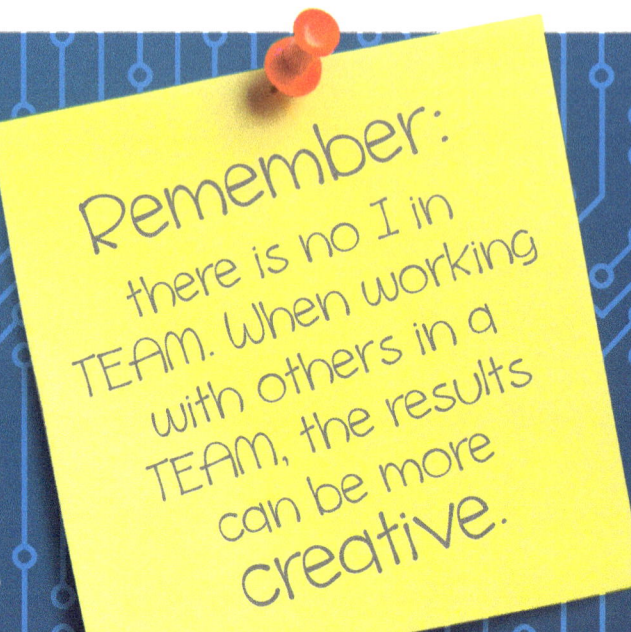

Remember: there is no I in TEAM. When working with others in a TEAM, the results can be more creative.

Introduction

You may ask, 'Why write a book about Design and Technology for primary students?' Design and Technology play a big role in our daily lives. From the time we wake up, to the time we go to bed, Design and Technology are part of our day. Some people also rely on Design and Technology while they are asleep.

So what is Design and Technology (or D&T)? Design and Technology are the problem-solving processes used to satisfy the needs of people, such as food, shelter, communication and travel. We use D&T to solve problems in our world. For example, using D&T, dams are built to store water for drinking, farming, hydroelectricity and future drought needs.

The significance of Design and Technology in our daily lives has been acknowledged by educators and presented as one of the areas of study in schools from Years 7 to 12, and more recently Prep to Year 6. The way to study D&T is to examine its building blocks. These building blocks help us to understand the *design and technology processes*. These processes enable individuals to use the same building blocks to solve problems in their daily lives with a view to the future.

Design and Technology in Today's World: A First Look introduces students to these building blocks. Students also learn to evaluate the design and technology processes used to produce items, systems or environments. The end results do not always guarantee benefits. Sometimes, there are significant costs to people and/or the Earth.

My aim is for everyone who uses this resource to gain technological literacy. That is, for students to develop the ability to use problem-solving and higher order thinking skills and then use these skills in the application of the design and technology processes to create, assess and communicate their solutions.

Professor Baz

I'm Professor Baz, your Design and Technology Mentor.

To the Teacher

This resource has two parts:
1. **eight units**
2. **eight activity sheets.**

Design and Technology in Today's World: A First Look introduces primary students from Year 3 to Year 6 to the building blocks of Design and Technology (D&T). These building blocks are presented as units of study supported by activity sheets.

The activity sheets contain a range of activities: individual research, small-group task(s) and/or classroom discussions. The classroom discussion activities are an opportunity to broaden the scope of the topic. They also provide a platform for addressing students' related interests as well as introducing any 'news-of-the-day' topics regarding design and technology. Teachers may adjust the topics and the scope of activities to suit different year levels and class needs.

Design and Technology in Today's World: A First Look is written to address the Years 3 & 4 and Years 5 & 6 bands of the *Australian Curriculum: Design and Technologies*, as well as individual states' and territories' Design and Technologies primary curricula. The units of study explore the strand 'Design and Technologies: Knowledge and Understanding', while the activity sheets explore the strand 'Design and Technologies: Processes and Production Skills'.

The following tables present an overview of the content descriptors of the *Australian Curriculum: Design and Technologies* and the related *Design and Technology in Today's World: A First Look* activity sheets. The activity sheets address the scope and sequence of the strands for Years 3 & 4 and Years 5 & 6.

Design and Technologies: Knowledge and Understanding

Technology & society

Years 3 & 4	Years 5 & 6
Recognise the role of people in design and technologies occupations and explore factors, including sustainability that impact on the design of products, services and environments to meet community needs (ACTDEK010)	Examine how people in design and technologies occupations address competing considerations, including sustainability in the design of products, services, and environments and for current and future use (ACTDEK019)

Years 3–6 Activity Sheets 1, 2, 6 and 7

Technologies contexts

Engineering principles and systems

Years 3 & 4	Years 5 & 6
Investigate how forces and the properties of materials affect the behaviour of a product or system (ACTDEK011)	Investigate how electrical energy can control movement, sound or light in a designed product or system (ACTDEK020)

Years 3–6 Activity Sheets 2, 3, 6A and 6B

Food and fibre production (Food specialisations)

Years 3 & 4	Years 5 & 6
Investigate food and fibre production and food technologies used in modern and traditional societies (ACTDEK012)	Investigate how and why food and fibre are produced in managed environments and prepared to enable people to grow and be healthy (ACTDEK021)

Years 3–6 Activity Sheet 6C

Materials and technologies specialisations

Years 3 & 4	Years 5 & 6
Investigate the suitability of materials, systems, components, tools and equipment for a range of purposes (ACTDEK013)	Investigate characteristics and properties of a range of materials, systems, components, tools and equipment and evaluate the impact of their use (ACTDEK023)

Years 3–6 Activity Sheets 3, 4, 5 and 6A

Source: http://docs.acara.edu.au/resources/Design_and_Technologies_-_Sequence_of_content.pdf

Design and Technologies: Processes and Production Skills

Creating designed solutions by:

Investigating and defining

Years 3 & 4	Years 5 & 6
Critique needs or opportunities for designing and explore and test a variety of materials, components, tools and equipment and the techniques needed to produce designed solutions (ACTDEP014)	Critique needs or opportunities for designing, and investigate materials, components, tools, equipment and processes to achieve intended designed solutions (ACTDEP024)

Years 3–6 Activity Sheets 1, 2, 3, 4, 5 and 7

Generating and designing

Years 3 & 4	Years 5 & 6
Generate, develop, and communicate design ideas and decisions using appropriate technical terms and graphical representation techniques (ACTDEP015)	Generate, develop, communicate and document design ideas and processes for audiences using appropriate technical terms and graphical representation techniques (ACTDEP025)

Years 3–6 Activity Sheet 2, 3, 4, 5 and 7

Producing and implementing

Years 3 & 4	Years 5 & 6
Select and use materials, components, tools, equipment and techniques and use safe work practices to make designed solutions (ACTDEP016)	Select appropriate materials, components, tools, equipment and techniques and apply safe procedures to make designed solutions (ACTDEP026)

Years 3–6 Activity Sheet 4, 5 and 8

Evaluating

Years 3 & 4	Years 5 & 6
Evaluate design ideas, processes and solutions based on criteria for success developed with guidance and including care for the environment (ACTDEP017)	Negotiate criteria for success that include sustainability to evaluate design ideas, processes and solutions (ACTDEP027)

Years 3–6 Activity Sheets 2, 7 and 8

Collaborating and managing

Years 3 & 4	Years 5 & 6
Plan a sequence of production steps when making designed solutions individually and collaboratively (ACTDEP018)	Develop project plans that include consideration of resources when making designed solutions individually and collaboratively (ACTDEP028)

Years 3–6 Activity Sheets 2, 3, 4, 6 and 6A

Source: http://docs.acara.edu.au/resources/Design_and_Technologies_-_Sequence_of_content.pdf

To the Student

Why study Design and Technology?

Design and Technology (D&T) is part of your world. Many of the everyday items that you use are the result of D&T. Learning about D&T will help you to understand why things are made the way they are. The knowledge you gain and the skills you develop will enable you to apply D&T processes to solve problems and create outcomes.

The content of this book looks at the building blocks of D&T. Each building block has two parts: a topic to explore and an activity to complete. Each activity sheet has a range of learning activities: individual research, a small group task(s) and/or a classroom discussion. Classroom discussions are your chance to learn more about D&T from each other. They are also an opportunity for you to raise points of interest that you wish to discuss. There are a few pages with lines/grids at the back of this book. These pages can be used to record extra notes and for sketching.

Your first activity will be to complete a '**KWL** Chart' before you start your D&T studies. The letter **K** stands for 'What do I **know** about Design and Technology?' The letter **W** stands for 'What **would** I like to know about Design and Technology?' The letter **L** stands for 'What have I **learnt** about Design and Technology?'

The KWL Chart is on the next page...

KWL Chart

Spend some time thinking about Design and Technology. What do you *know* about Design and Technology? What *would* you like to know about Design and Technology?

Now complete the 'What do I *know* about Design and Technology?' column. Then complete the 'What *would* I like to know about Design and Technology?' column.

You will complete the 'What have I *learnt* about Design and Technology?' column at the end of your studies.

What do I *know* about Design and Technology?	What *would* I like to know about Design and Technology?	What have I *learnt* about Design and Technology?

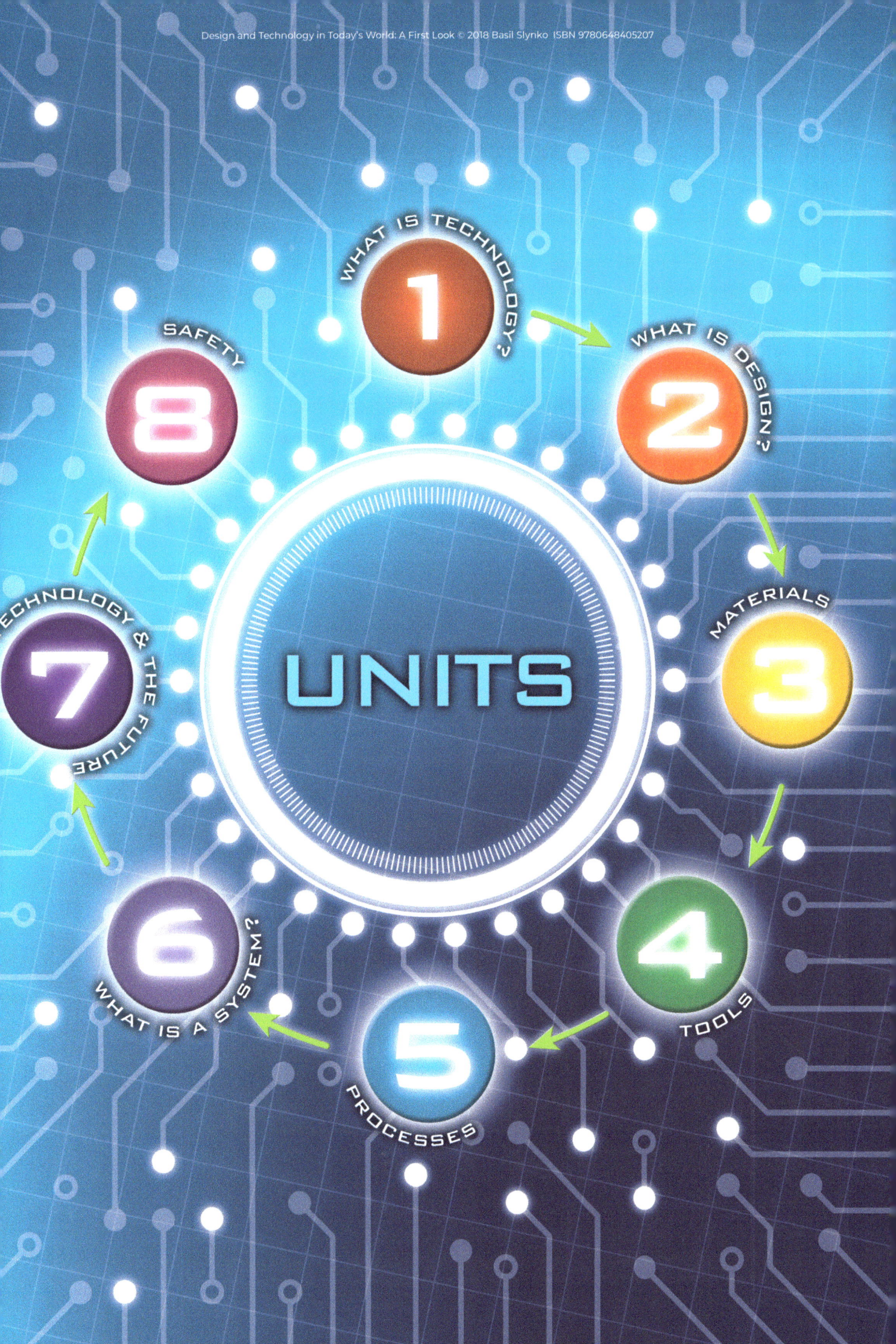

1. What is technology?

What comes to your mind when you hear the word '**technology**'? Like many people, you may think of computers, smartphones, tablets, MP3s, digital cameras and other 'high-tech' items. The term 'high tech' was first used in the 1970s.

High tech, or **high technology**, is technology based on scientific and technical knowledge. This knowledge is so advanced that it is beyond the understanding of untrained people. An example is **microelectronics**.

What is the meaning of technology? A dictionary is a good place to look. Here are some examples of the primary (first) meanings of technology as listed in dictionaries:

> **technology (tek-nol-uh-jee), noun**
> 1. the study of machinery, engineering, and how things work,
>   *The Australian Integrated School Dictionary and Thesaurus*, 2002.
> 2. an area of science that studies and uses practical ways of doing things,
>   *First Australian Dictionary & Thesaurus* 2010.

Well, were you surprised to read these meanings? Are they what you expected to read?

Another meaning of technology is:
- people using resources such as:

  `IDEAS` `INFORMATION` `SKILLS` `MATERIALS` `ENERGY` `TOOLS & EQUIPMENT`

  and
- a problem-solving process such as:

Look into: *exploring how to solve the problem and considering the impacts on people and the environment.*

Plan: *coming up with a detailed way to make an item.*

Create: *making the item using materials, tools and processes.*

Assess: *testing the item and researching its effect on people and the environment.*

- to produce **a satisfactory solution to a problem.**

Digital technology

Technology is based on a body of knowledge. Knowledge is often grouped and divided into branches.

Construction technology

Communication technology

Transportation technology

2 What is design?

Design is the process of planning an outcome (a result). The outcome could be making an item such as a toy or a piece of clothing. The outcome could also be a system that lets you know when someone opens a door.

Designing is a problem-solving activity. This activity may be done by one person or a group of people working together, as in industry. Designing is usually the basis of all technology.

Look into: *exploring how to solve the problem and considering the impacts on people and the environment.*

Plan: *coming up with a detailed way to make an item.*

Create: *making the item using materials, tools and processes.*

Assess: *testing the item and researching its effect on people and the environment.*

A problem-solving process

Using a problem-solving process ensures that the solution will be the best possible solution, within certain limits.
For example, the solution should:
- be easy to use
- be safe to use
- not cost too much
- be able to last for a period of time
- not harm the environment
- look good.

The solution will look good if it has a pleasing shape. The shape can be improved by the use of colour. Colour usually adds to the look. The overall look is known as **visual appeal**. Visual appeal is often what we first notice.

A good design is something that:
- people want to use
- does no harm to people
- does no damage to the Earth.

The problem-solving process can be very complex. There is much to think about. Many decisions need to be made. One way to make the problem-solving process easier is to use smaller steps.

Let's have a look at a design process using smaller steps.

Do these items have visual appeal? Why or why not?

A design process: How it works

continues ...

3 Materials

A **material** is a substance that can be used to make something else. A common material is wood. For example, wood can be used to build furniture and homes or for wood turning.

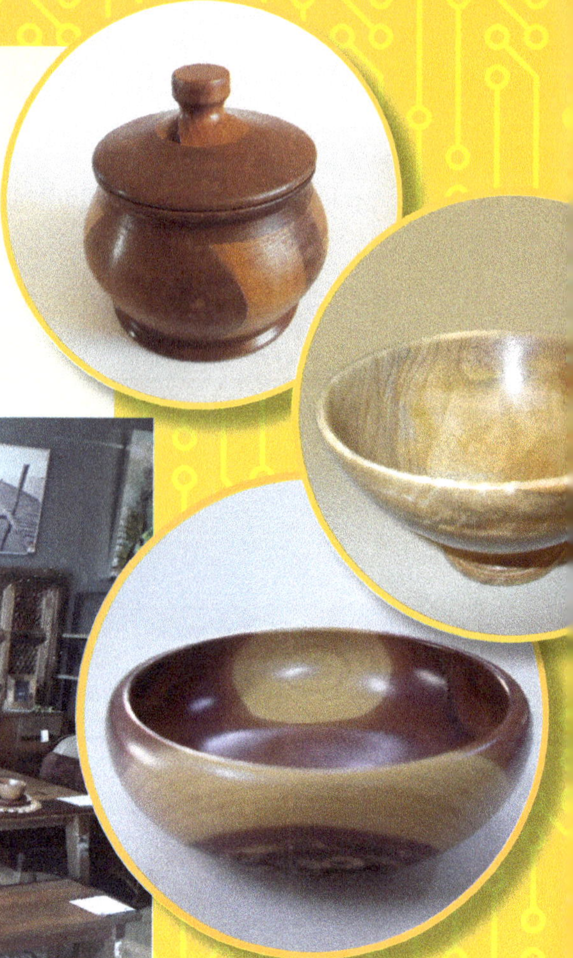

Wood used for furniture

Examples of items made by wood turning

Look at the photographs below. How many materials can you name? What do you know about these materials?

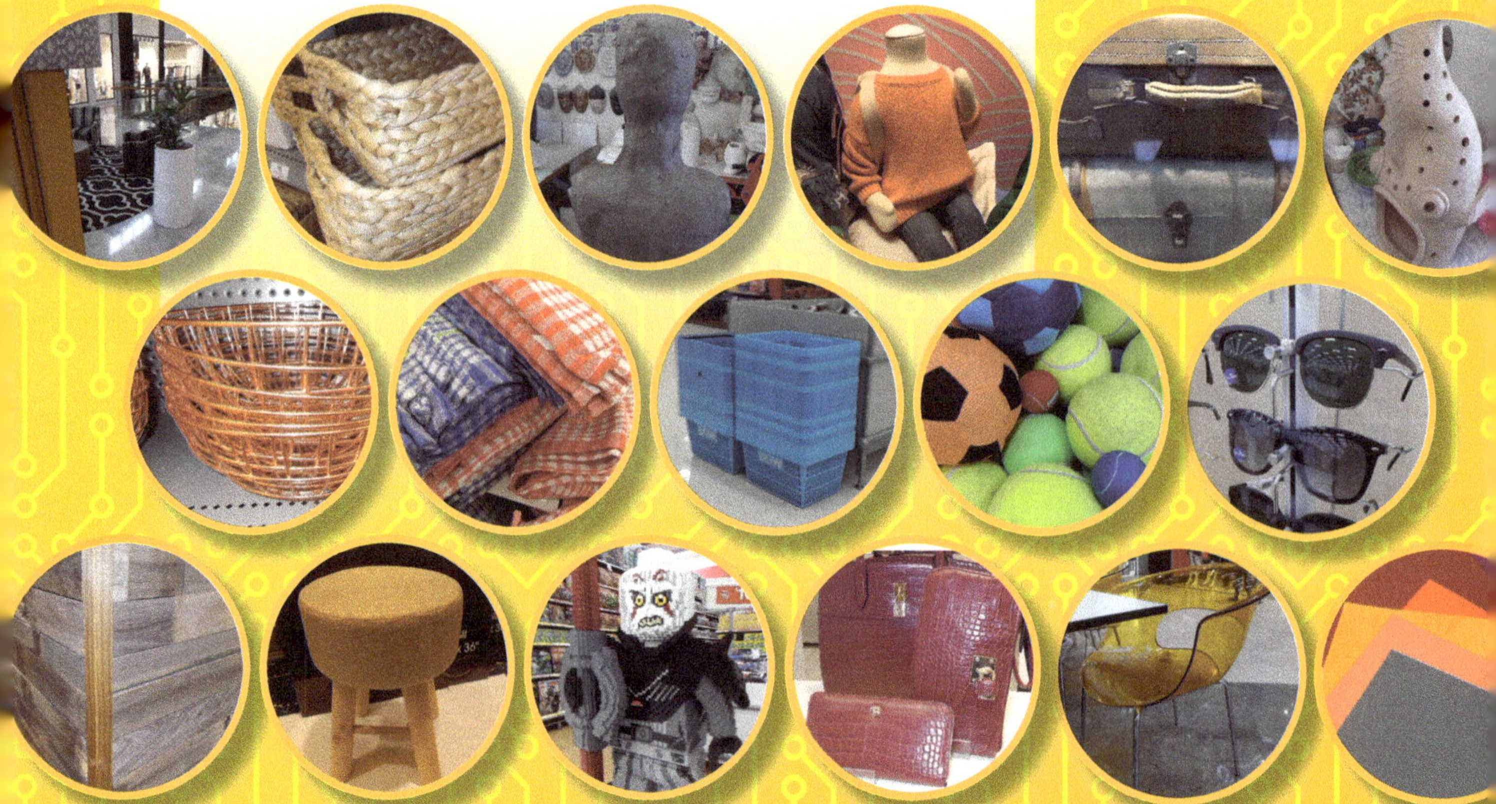

Materials can be sorted into four basic groups: natural, processed, synthetic and composite.

Here are some samples of materials from each group.

Natural – found in nature
- Wood
- Stone
- Straw
- Cork
- Mud

Processed – usually using natural materials
- Ore → steel
- Bauxite → aluminium
- Plant or animal fibres → fabric
- Clay → ceramics

Synthetic – made from chemicals
- Acrylic sheeting
- Polystyrene
- Epoxy resin
- Polyester resin

Composite – combining two or more materials
- Brass = copper + zinc
- Cob = clay + sand + straw
- Concrete = sand + stones + cement + water
- Gore-Tex® = fabric + plastic film + thin layer of foam

3

Different materials are used for different things. Have you wondered why? It is to do with the **properties** of materials. Each material has its own set of properties. These properties determine how a material should be used. For example, wood is strong when squeezed (**compression**) and steel is strong when stretched (**tension**).

Some properties of materials:

Hardness
How well does it resist denting or scratching?

Strength
How easy or difficult is it to break?

Toughness
How much force can it stand without breaking?

Elasticity
How well does it return to its original shape and size after being subjected to external loads and forces?

Density
How heavy or light is it for its size?

Flammability
How easily does it burn or smoulder when exposed to heat or fire?

Conductivity
How well does it conduct or insulate against heat, electricity or sound?

Durability
How well does it resist environmental stresses such as weather or insects, or does it tear easily or wear out (e.g. fabric)?

10

Tools

Tools have been designed to enable people to complete tasks more easily. For example, you could use a small rock to drive a nail into timber, but it is easier and more comfortable to use a hammer.

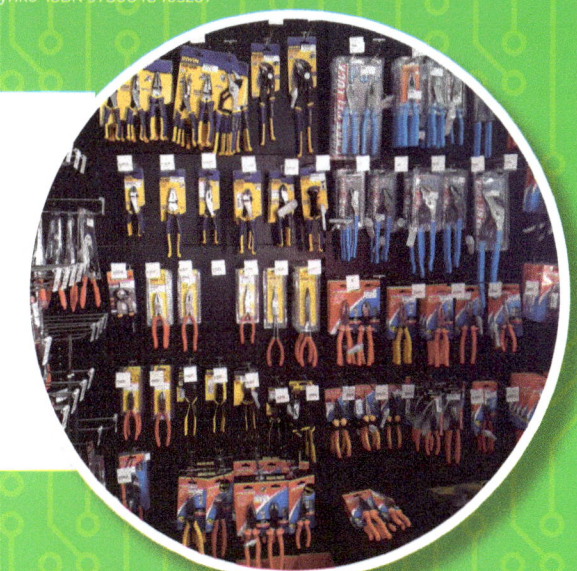

Did you know that there are **four main groups of tools?**

- Hand tools
  - Claw hammer
  - Locking pliers
  - General-purpose saw
- Portable power tools
  - Cordless drill driver
  - Jig saw
  - Circular saw
- Industrial equipment
  - Industrial robot
  - Tunnel boring machine
  - Hydraulic press
- Universal equipment
  - Pedestal drill press
  - Disc sander
  - CNC laser cutting machine

4

Tools have been designed over the years to perform new tasks. Some tools have been adapted over time to use new energy sources. Electricity saw the development of power tools and universal equipment. Cordless power tools have changed the way things are done today.

Let's have a look at some common tools that you might use.

Cordless power tools

Marking-out/measuring tools
Used to draw a shape(s) to size

1. **Steel rule**
2. **Folding rule**
3. **Flexible tape**
4. **Try-square**

Cutting tools
Used to cut materials to size and shape

Knives and scissors are used for cutting soft and flexible materials such as paper, cardboard, plastic or rubber.

5. Craft knife; 6. Snap-blade knife; 7. Traditional trimming scissors

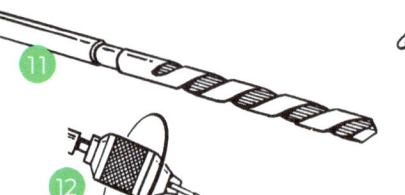

←Twist drill

Saws can be used to cut straight lines or curves in wood, plastics or soft metal.

8. Tenon saw; 9. Coping saw; 10. Junior hacksaw

Drills are used for making holes in solid materials such as wood, metal or plastics.

11. Twist drill; 12. A tool holder is used to spin the tool

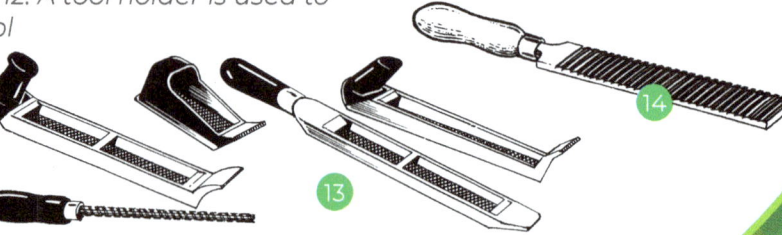

Files are used for shaping or removing timber, metal or plastic waste.

13. Surform tools; 14. Hand file

4

Hitting tools
Used to strike another tool or thing

15. Warrington hammer;
16. Soft-faced hammer; 17. Mallet;
18. Claw hammer

Clamping & holding devices
Used to provide a temporary force to hold items

19. Quick-grip clamp;
20. Spring clamps;
21. Webbing clamp

Torsion (twisting) tools
Used to provide a twisting or turning force

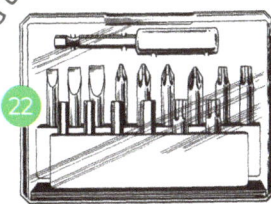

22. Interchangeable screwdriver bits (used with a handle)

Portable power tools & universal equipment
These are a great help because they save you time.

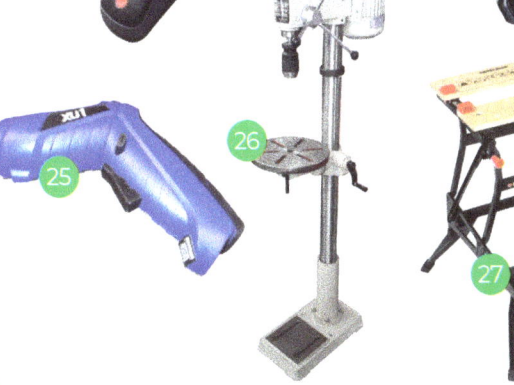

23. Cordless glue gun; 24. Cordless drill driver;
25. Cordless screwdriver; 26. Pedestal drill press; 27. Workmate®

TAKE CARE WHEN USING TOOLS! You can injure yourself or someone else. *(See Unit 8: Safety.)*

5 Processes

People use tools and equipment to process materials. Materials are sold in a range of shapes and sizes to meet the different demands of industry and people. These various shapes and sizes are known as **stock materials**.

Stock materials can be altered using one of three processes: forming, separating or combining.

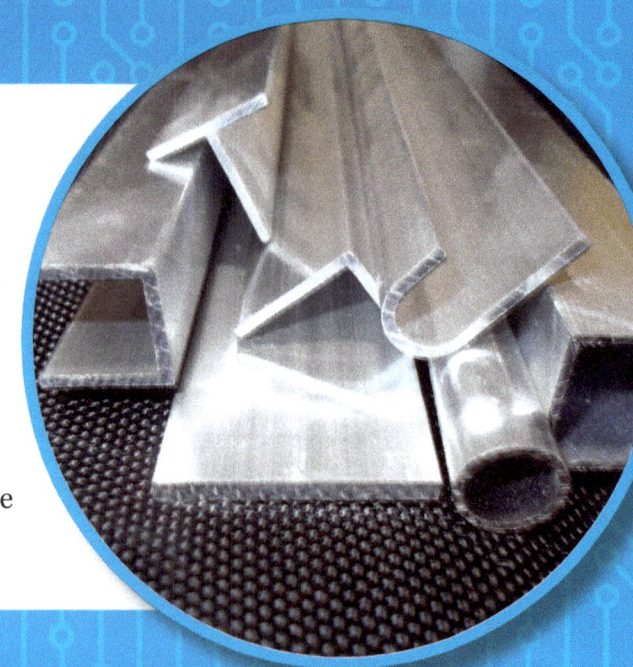

Some common shapes of stock materials

Forming

Forming is the process of changing the shape of a material. No material is removed during this process.

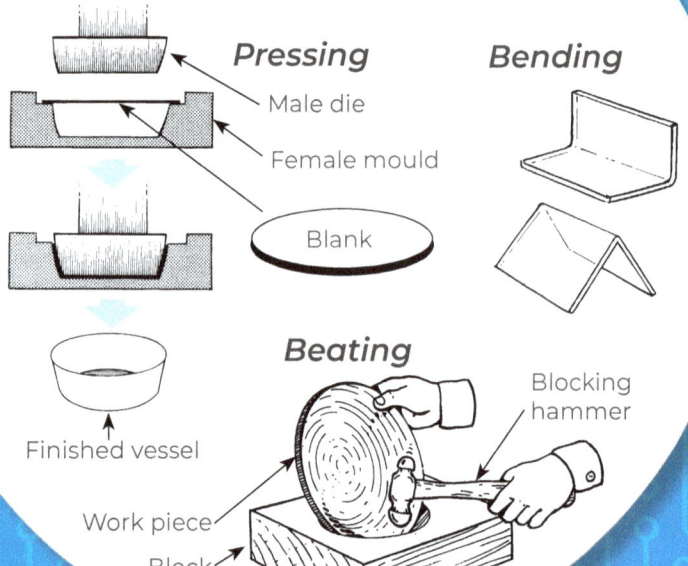

Some common forming processes

Separating

Separating is the process of removing part of the material from a piece of material.

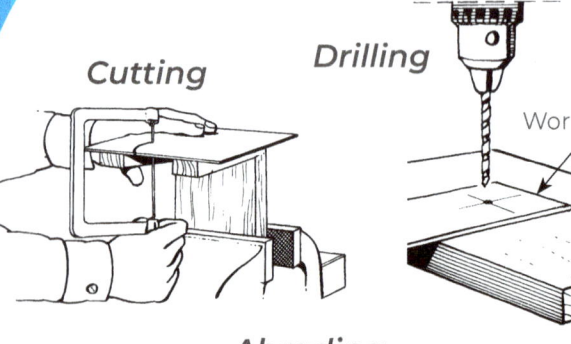

Abrading
Use a cork block with abrasive paper – it extends the life of the paper.

Some common separating processes

Reducing waste material is often a challenge.
Here is what you should do when marking out shapes:
- Use the edge(s) where possible.
- Leave the smallest gap possible between shapes.
- Place your shape(s) as close as possible to the edge(s).

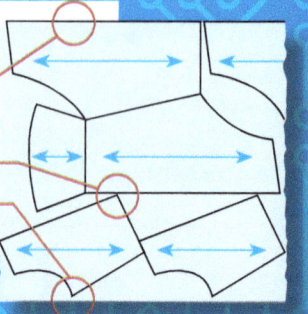

Make sure you position patterns to ensure minimal wastage.

Combining

Combining is the process of joining two or more materials. The materials can be the same or different. Note that the combining process can be either *permanent* or *semi-permanent*.

Two common ways of combining materials is using glues and fasteners.

Glues and adhesives

Mechanical fasteners

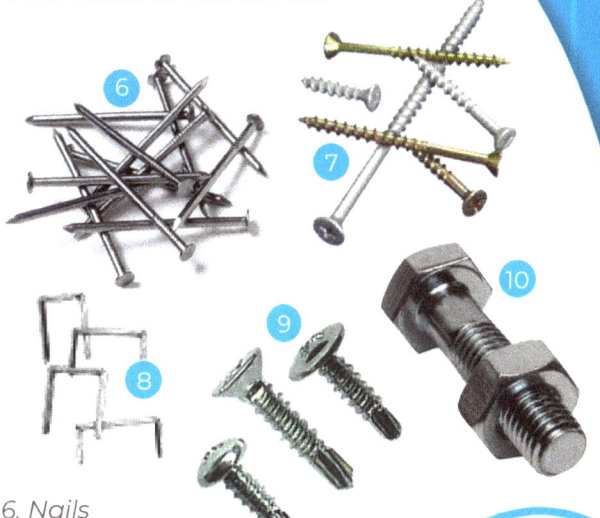

6. Nails
7. Screws
8. Staples
9. Self-tapping screws
10. Bolts and nuts

Pull-apart fasteners

11. Quick-release buckles
12. Press studs
13. Zips

1. Paste – use for paper or cardboard
2. PVA glue – use for timber, paper, cardboard or fabric
3. Contact cement – use for various materials (read the instructions)
4. Hot-melt gun – a range of glue sticks is available to use with different materials
5. Tapes (sticky, duct, masking) – a quick and easy way to join many materials. Some tapes can be easily removed; for example, masking tape.

Examples of glues, adhesives and fasteners

People did not always use glues and fasteners. Materials have been combined over time using string, rope or vines. Many natural materials can be combined using stitching, lacing or lashing.

Sewing leather using a running stitch

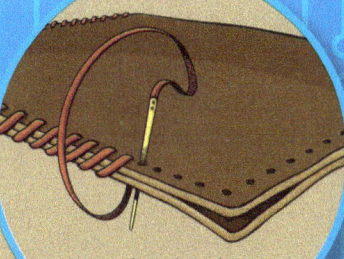

Sewing leather with a thong

6 What is a system?

Do you know what a system is?

> **system (sis-tem), noun**
> a set of parts, things or ideas that work together
> *First Australian Dictionary & Thesaurus* 2010.

A **system** is another way to create an outcome or complete a task.

These are the basic parts of a system:

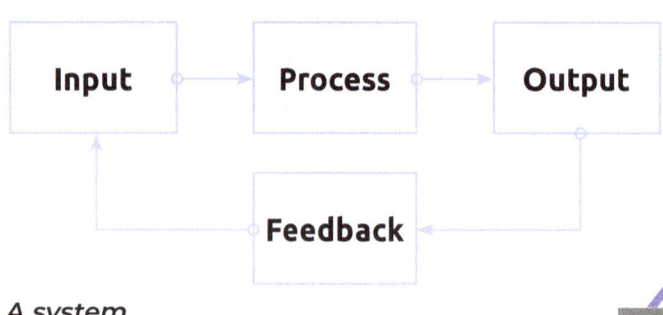

A system

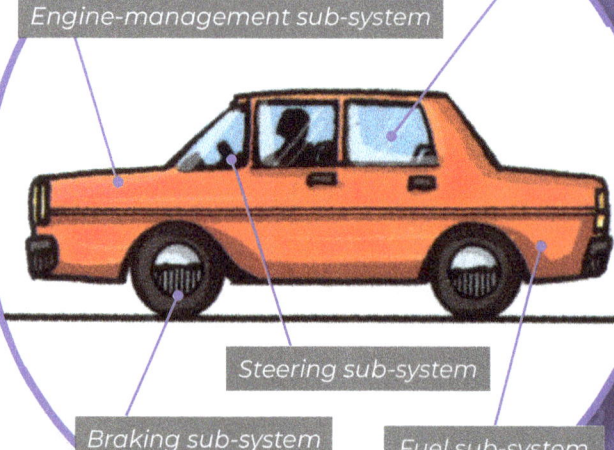

Examples of sub-systems in a vehicle

- Climate-control sub-system
- Engine-management sub-system
- Steering sub-system
- Braking sub-system
- Fuel sub-system

- The **input** is any resource that contributes to a system, such as information, people, materials and tools.

- The **process** is all the activities done to produce the result.

- The **output** is the result or goal and its impacts. The impacts may be benefits or costs.

- The **feedback** is the information – positive or negative – about the output. More resources may be required to improve the output.

Our world is full of systems. Examples are communication systems, transportation systems and manufacturing systems.

Systems are usually made up of a number of sub-systems. Each **sub-system** has its own input, process, output and feedback. Sub-systems may also use lower sub-systems that work together to produce the output.

We will look at three systems. They are:
- technological systems
- agricultural systems
- control systems.

Can you think of some other sub-system in a vehicle?

Technological systems

Technological systems solve problems and produce an outcome.

Let's have a look at two technological systems: manufacturing systems and construction systems.

1 Manufacturing systems

A **manufacturing system** enables people to make items that they want and avoid delays.

```
Input                    Process                            Output
Information              Investigating what people want     Product
Materials                Developing the item                Waste
Tools and equipment      Producing the item
Skills                   Marketing and sales

                         Feedback
                         Quality
                         Wastage
```

A manufacturing system

Manufacturing systems can mass produce an item such as a mobile phone or make a specific item such as a gas storage tank for an energy supplier. Other manufacturing systems may make one part of an item, such as a screen for a mobile phone. This screen is sold to a manufacturer, who assembles the mobile phone.

Manufacturing systems often use computers to design and test items before making them. This process is known as **computer-aided design (CAD)**. The CAD software can model the designed item and test it. Any changes to the design can be made quickly, before it is produced.

Computers also control the machines that are used to make these items. These machines can repeat the task over and over to make many identical parts. This process is known as **computer-aided manufacturing (CAM)**.

The combined process is known as **CAD/CAM**.

A gas storage tank

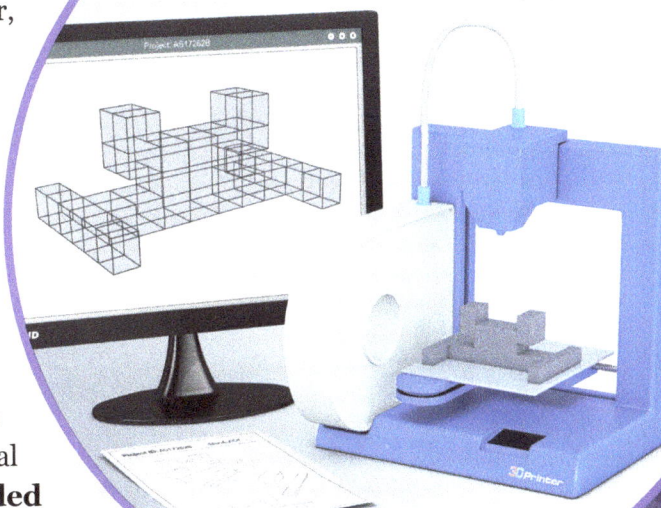

A CAD/CAM system

2 Construction systems

A **construction system** enables people to plan and build structures in an organised way and avoid delays.

Input
Discussing the needs of clients
Presenting plans
Seeking approval

Process
Preparing the construction site
Building the structure
Restoring the site

Output
Using the structure

Feedback
Faults
Problems

A construction system

A **structure** is a thing that can carry a load and withstand other forces acting on it. There are two types of structures:
- a frame
- a shell.

Structures are built to:
- provide shelter, e.g. buildings
- control the environment, e.g. dams
- carry loads, e.g. bridges.

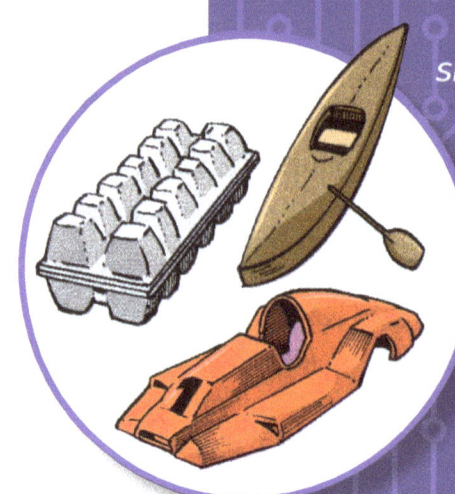

Frame structures: a frame structure made of triangular shapes. A triangle is a more rigid (not easily bent) shape.

Shell structures have no frame, but they have an outside skin.

How many structures can you see in this illustration?

Agricultural systems

Agricultural systems feed and clothe us.

Agricultural systems enable people to produce food and fibre in an organised way.

Input	Process	Output
Soil	Planting and/or breeding	Food produce
Seeds	Fertilising and/or feeding	and/or animals
Animals	Harvesting	Fibre
Water	Selling	Waste

Feedback
Quantity
Quality
Wastage
Impacts on environment

An agricultural system

There are three basic agricultural systems. They are:
- mixed-farm agricultural systems
- extensive agricultural systems
- intensive agricultural systems.

Mixed-farm agricultural systems use land to produce a combination of food or fibre such as wheat (sheep), dairy (pigs) or beef (grain).

Extensive agricultural systems use large areas of land to produce food or fibre. Examples are a cattle station or a cotton farm.

Intensive agricultural systems use much less land, but require more money to set up and produce food or fibre. Examples are a piggery or a hydroponic farm.

Agricultural systems are supported by sub-systems such as a soil sub-system, a plant sub-system or an animal sub-system. Each sub-system, and lower sub-systems, contribute to the quantity and quality of the output.

Basic agricultural sub-systems

Cotton farming

Hydroponic farming

6c Control systems

Control systems complete tasks in an organised way.

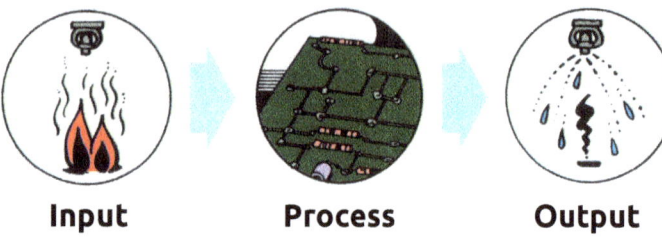

Input → Process → Output

There are two kinds of control systems:
- open-loop
- closed-loop.

An **open-loop control system** has no way of checking its output because there is no feedback.

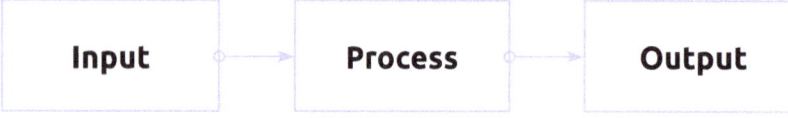

An open-loop control system

A **closed-loop control system** has a way of checking its output. It can check the output because of feedback. This system can stop the output even after the action is done.

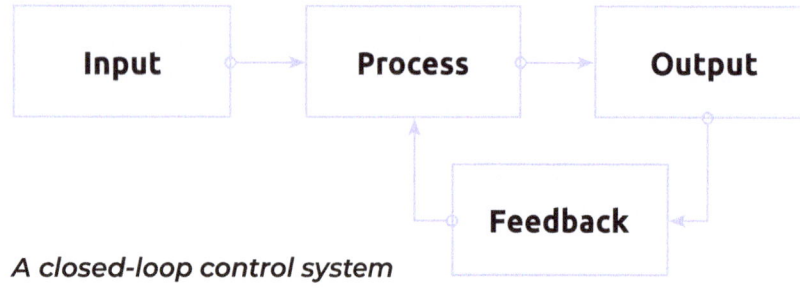

A closed-loop control system

Many control systems use computers to monitor the system and make adjustments. These adjustments can be made by using mechanisms, hydraulics and/or electrical signals.

Mechanisms transmit force and movement to produce a result.

Hydraulics use liquids such as water or oil to transmit force and movement.

Electrical signals use circuits to produce an output such as light, sound or movement. A **circuit** is a continuous loop made up of various **components** that can carry an electrical current.

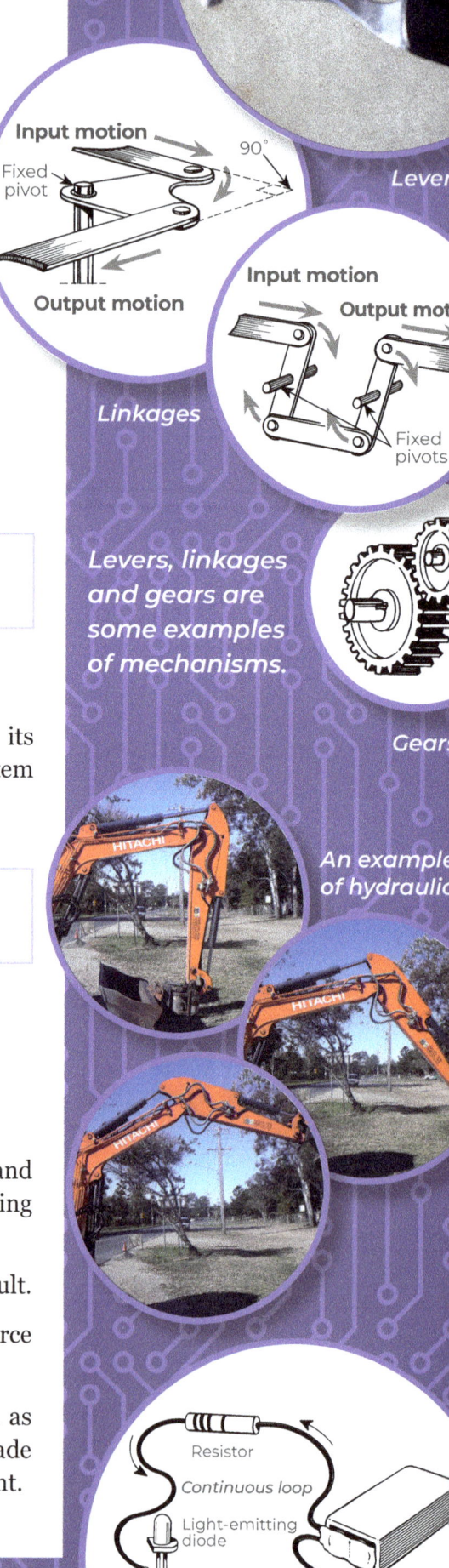

Levers, linkages and gears are some examples of mechanisms.

An example of hydraulic

A simple circuit

7 Technology and the future

Our world has seen huge changes in many areas since the year 2000. The expanding memory of computers and modelling software is enabling people to design and produce some amazing things. Designers and engineers are able to test an idea using a computer before making the finished product.

Our world relies greatly on energy – both renewable and non-renewable. The interest in **renewable energy** is growing as the result of the **greenhouse gases debate**.

Our 'throw-away' approach is polluting the Earth. Landfill sites are being chocked with waste. Our oceans are chocked with plastics. The challenge is to recycle things and materials when designing outcomes.

There is also a greater need for sustainable development. **Sustainability** is about considering the welfare not only of ourselves, but also of future generations and the Earth's future. It is about having a long-term view of life instead of only considering personal gain at the expense of others and the environment.

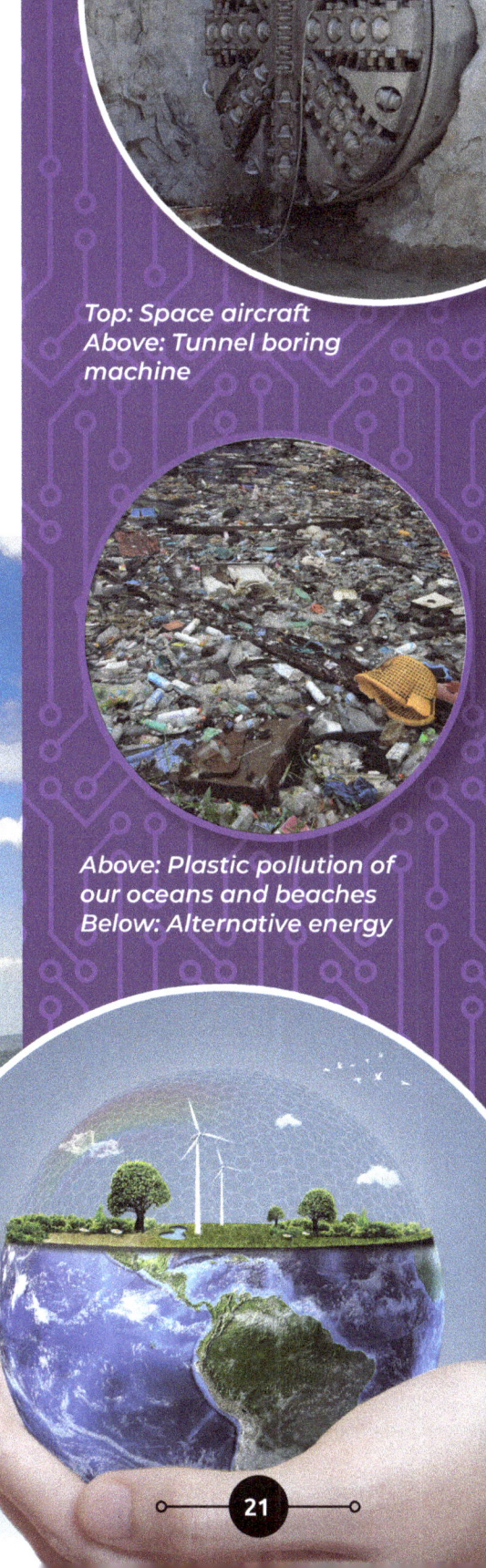

Top: Space aircraft
Above: Tunnel boring machine

Above: Plastic pollution of our oceans and beaches
Below: Alternative energy

Taipei 101 is one of the world's tallest buildings.

We live in an exciting world. What's next?

7

Technology will continue to shape our world and benefit us. However, the big issue is the cost of technology; that is, its impact on people and the environment. The costs, in some cases, have been greater than the benefits.

One of the costs of technology is the loss of jobs. Some jobs have disappeared due to technological advances; for example, people have been replaced by robots and computer-controlled machines that perform dangerous tasks. Much of the physical work on construction sites is also now done by industrial equipment.

Some of the jobs that you might be considering as your career could also become redundant as technology continues to shape the future. However, emerging technologies will provide new job opportunities.

There is always a place for a person who can:
- think about an issue
- evaluate a situation
- adapt an outcome to solve a need
- communicate with others
- work with others.

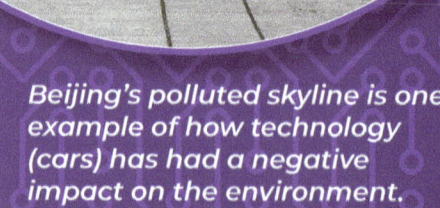

Beijing's polluted skyline is one example of how technology (cars) has had a negative impact on the environment.

Industrial robots in a factory

Safety

Safety is about stopping something bad from happening to you and those around you; for example, cutting your finger(s) when using a knife, falling off a stool or dropping an item onto someone's toes. Accidents can happen anywhere, any time: in the home, on the sports field or at school. Be aware!

We all need to be reminded about safety rules. Safety rules are often seen on posters and signs to remind us to be safe and to wear safety gear.

Safety rules are there to protect people. You should:
- read the safety rules
- understand the safety rules
- obey the safety rules
- use the safety gear.

Personal Protective Equipment (PPE) is the general term used to describe safety gear.

Safety is an important part of all design and technology activities. As part of your technology studies, you will plan and create items using materials, tools and processes. Many tools and materials have sharp edges, so handle them with care. When you use a tool or a piece of equipment to complete a process for the first time, take special care. Make sure you know how to complete the process safely. Finally, always use safety gear such as glasses, gloves and hair nets to protect your body.

Personal safety is all about four letters – **TUAT**:
- *Think* before you act
- *Use* PPE
- *Ask* (if you're unsure)
- *Then* do.

'TUAT' will keep you safe.

It is important to read and observe safety banners and posters.

Some examples of safety signs include:

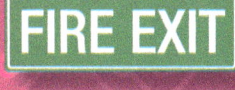

Some examples of Personal Protective Equipment (PPE)

Find-a-word

Can you find all 85 technology-related words in the grid below?

```
E X T S N O I T A R E D I S N O C Q A J W E M H C
L N H F A V S U S T A I N A B I L I T Y V A A H K
E D O G Y C O L L O B O R A T I O N H H L D T N A
C R U N E G N I D L I U B P O L E V E D J B E E G
T O G I X R T U P T U O W P M M C E F U T U R E R
R B H N P R E P A R A T I O N O I S S U C S I D I
I O T R A Z E C L C O M P O N E N T S F R N A S C
C T S A N T I S A A P D R L Q J I I E L D N L B U
I I D E S F U J O A C I U H U N R G T U O K S E L
T C F L I L P R C U V I T C G S H A S O R O G E T
Y S K C O T V T A N R G N I T S E T A O R K T M U
M G E I N R I U E L O C S H Q I R I W I H I E K R
J P R T N H T V O A R I E T C Y O O I O S S N M E
S O H E T P G N I D N A T S R E D N U O U O F G E
I L E H N E U W O T H E C A M U T T P A W L W C X
N L S T E E C T E C C S G O R E C M C L H U O H T
T U U N M V W H S H H A D A N O O T E P C T R A E
E T O Y P S R A N O A E B S M C L D U J R I L N N
G I H S I E U I B O L I I E V S G P P R A O D G S
R O N M U Q Q U Z L L V S A F E T Y X H E N I E I
A N E E Q U S Q I I E O I K N P R O C E S S E S V
T T E T E E X N T A N O G N I N N A L P E O P L E
I A R S S N G Y N T G R K Y G L R B C D R X G A P
O U G Y K C A B D E E F F E C T L I T E N S I O N
N T A S A E D I K D M E C H A N I S A T I O N G X
```

ACTIVITIES	DISCUSSION	INTEGRATION	POLLUTION	SYNTHETIC
ADJUSTING	DURABILITY	INTENSIVE	PPE	SYSTEMS
AGRICULTURE	EFFECT	INVESTIGATION	PREPARATION	TECHNICAL
AIR	ELECTRICITY	KNOWLEDGE	PROCESSES	TECHNIQUES
BUILDING	ENERGY	LEARNING	PRODUCTION	TECHNOLOGY
CARE	ENVIRONMENT	LOOP	RENEWABLE	TENSION
CAUSE	EQUIPMENT	GREENHOUSE	RESEARCH	TESTING
CHALLENGE	EXPANSION	MATERIALS	RESOURCES	THOUGHTS
CHANGE	EXPLORATION	MECHANISATION	ROBOTICS	TOOLS
COLLABORATION	EXTENSIVE	MODELLING	SAFETY	TOY
COMPONENTS	FEEDBACK	MONITORING	SEQUENCE	TUAT
COMPOSITE	FUTURE	NATURAL	SKILLS	UNDERSTANDING
CONSIDERATIONS	GOALS	NEEDS	SOLUTIONS	USES
CONTROL	IDEAS	OUTCOMES	SOLVING	WASTE
DESIGN	IMPACT	OUTPUT	SPECIFICATIONS	WATER
DETAIL	INDUSTRY	PEOPLE	STRUCTURES	WORK
DEVELOP	INPUT	PLANNING	SUSTAINABILITY	WORLD

See page 60 for the solution.

AS 1 What is technology?

High-tech items have changed a great deal since the 1970s. For example, look at an early mobile phone and movie camera.

1986 Racal phone   Early movie camera

Q1. Select one of the items illustrated.

The item I have selected is _____

Q2. What do you notice about the item? Write some of your first thoughts below.

_____
_____
_____

Q3. Select a digital technology item that you use today, other than a mobile phone or movie camera.

My digital technology item is _____ . It was released in 20_____ . [year]

Q3a. Do an internet image search of the digital technology item you chose.
Sketch the image below. Then answer the questions. You may need to carry out some research.

What is the size of the item? _____ x _____ x _____

What is its weight? _____

What is it able to do? _____
_____
_____
_____

My digital technology item

Q3b. Now do an internet image search of the original model of the item you chose.
Sketch the image below. Then answer the questions. You may need to carry out some research.

What is the size of the item? _____ x _____ x _____

What is its weight? _____

What was it able to do? _____
_____
_____
_____

Original model

Class discussion

Q4. Many digital technology items have become smaller in size and can do more than their earlier versions. Discuss and write down some of the reasons for this.

_____
_____
_____

Q5. Present a timeline for the digital technology item that you selected in Question 3. Use the internet to research the details of each model. Sketch an image of each model.

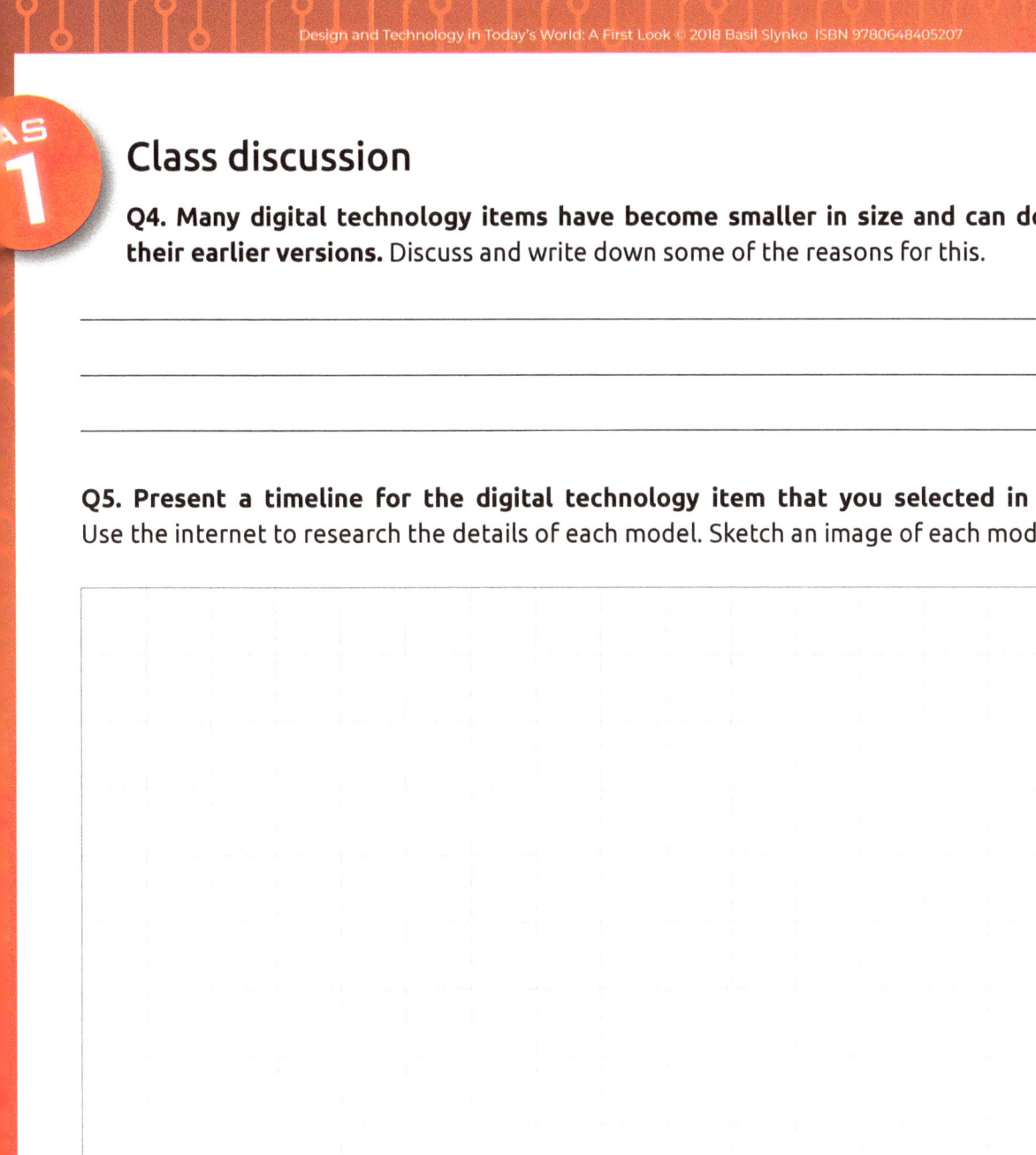

AS 2 What is design?

One way to understand design is to analyse items. You can then assess items to decide how well the designs have worked and their impact on people and the Earth. For example, you may find that:

- some designs could be improved
- other materials could have been used
- product waste is a problem
- the item is unsafe
- the item did not last for a long period of time
- the item is not easy to use.

There is a large range of toys designed for children of different ages. Each toy has a role to play in children's development.

Children's toys

Q1. Select one of the toys shown here. Then answer the questions below.

The toy I selected is

_____ .

Q1a. Does it look good?

Yes ☐ No ☐   Describe the toy: _____

_____

Q1b. Is it easy to use?

Yes ☐ No ☐   Why/why not? _____

_____

_____

Q1c. Will it last for a long time?

Yes ☐ No ☐   Why/why not? _____

_____

_____

Q1d. Does it harm people or the environment?

Yes ☐ No ☐   Why/why not? _____

_____

_____

Q1e. Write down the improvements that could be made to this toy.

_____

_____

_____

_____

_____

Small-group activity

Q2. Find other students who have chosen the same toy. Compare your responses. Add any comments below that you did not record in Question 1.

_____
_____
_____

Q3. You have been asked to design a soft toy for toddlers. Use the space below to draw your toy. Things to consider are:

☐ materials ☐ visual appeal ☐ size ☐ shape ☐ personal safety ☐ damage to the environment

Write down a name for your toy that could be used to market it. _____

AS 3 Materials

A material is a substance that can be used to make something. Each material has its own set of properties. These properties determine how a material should be used.

Strength
How easy or difficult is it to break?

Toughness
How much force can it stand without breaking?

Hardness
How well does it resist denting or scratching?

Elasticity
How well does it return to its original shape and size after being subjected to external loads and forces?

Density
How heavy or light is it for its size?

Conductivity
How well does it conduct or insulate against heat, electricity or sound?

Flammability
How easily does it burn or smoulder when exposed to heat or fire?

Durability
How well does it resist environmental stresses such as weather or insects, or does it tear easily or wear out (e.g. fabric)?

Q1. Look at the illustrations above and think about the properties of each material listed in the table below. Record some of these properties in the *Main properties* column.

Then use the internet to check your choice of properties for each material. Correct any wrong choices and add any properties that you did not record. Complete the rest of the table by writing in each material's uses and weaknesses.

Materials and their main properties, uses and weaknesses

Material	Main properties	Use(s)	Weakness(es)
Wood			
Aluminium			
Cardboard			

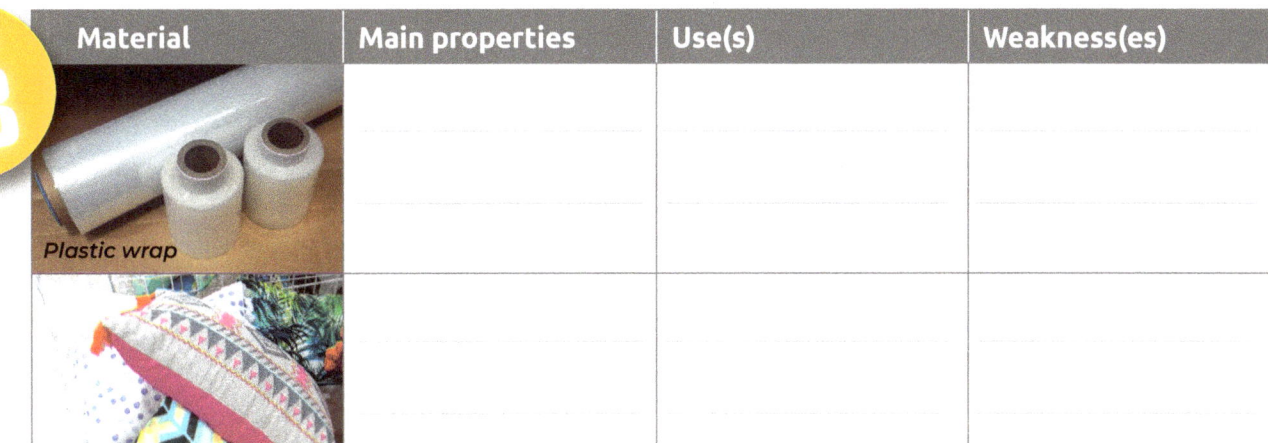

Material	Main properties	Use(s)	Weakness(es)
Plastic wrap			
Fabric			

Materials are sold in standard sizes. These materials are known as stock materials. For example, the size of acrylic sheeting is 2400 mm × 1200 mm or 1800 mm × 1200 mm and it is available in various thicknesses.

Small-group activity

Q2. Use the internet to investigate some of the standard sizes of stock materials illustrated in the table below. Write your findings in the table. *Hint*: Search the websites of trade centres, timber suppliers, hardware stores and sewing or craft stores.

Material	Size	Some stock sizes available
Sawn timber		a x b (exclude length)
Aluminium sheet		a x b (exclude thickness)
Steel rod		Diameter a (exclude length)
Cardboard		a x b (exclude thickness)
Fabric		a x b (exclude thickness)

4. Tools

Tools have been designed to enable people to complete tasks more easily. Tools are often made in different sizes for a range of uses; for example, a mini hammer and a sledge hammer, or a watchmaker's screwdriver and an engineer's screwdriver.

Q1. Using the Tool Bank, select a tool that you would use to complete each of the processes shown below. Write the number of the tool in the box next to the correct process.

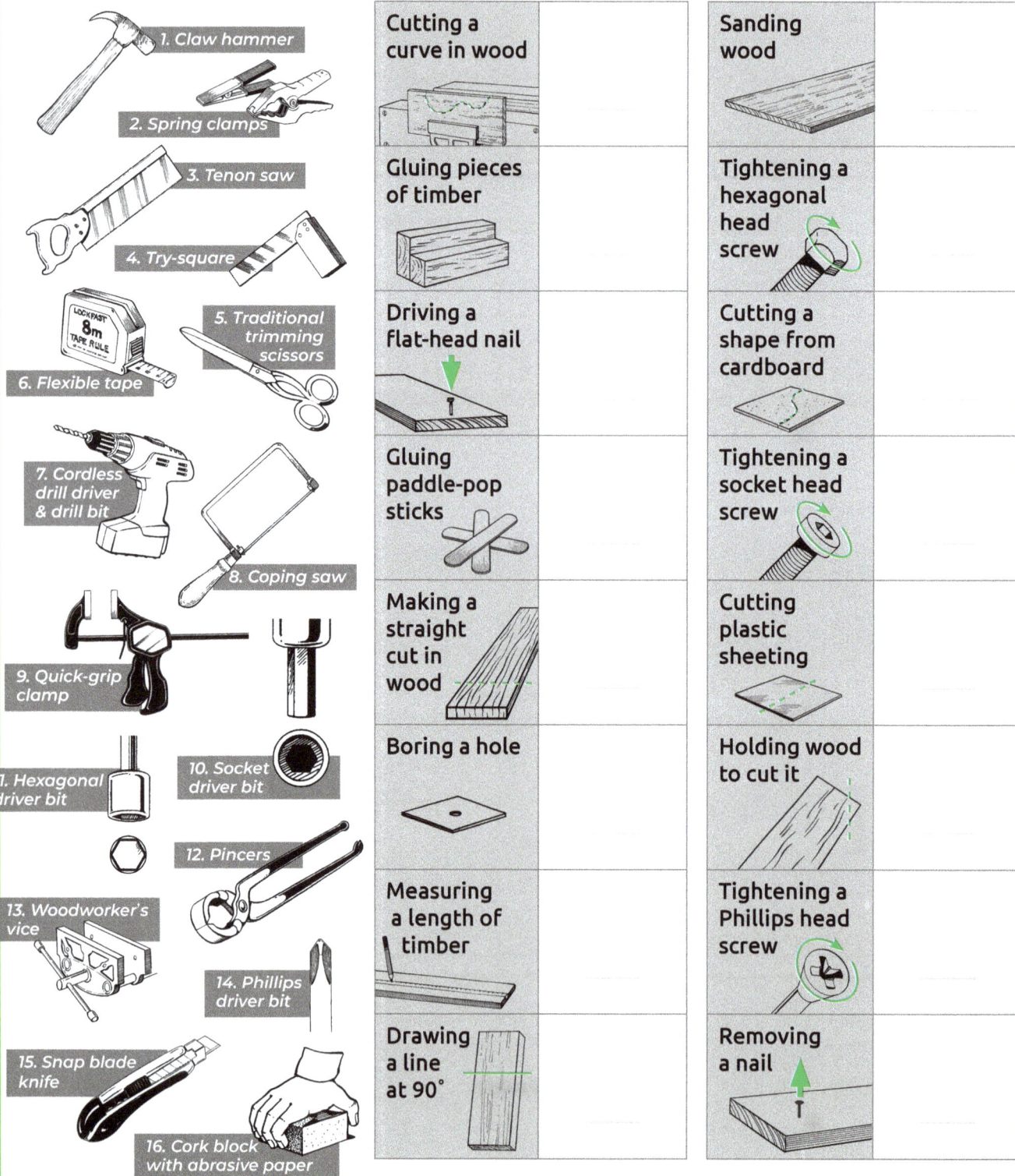

Small-group activity

Q2. What other tools could you use for some of the processes in Question 1?
Select three processes and then complete this table.

The processes I have selected are:	Other tools that I could use are:
1.	
2.	
3.	

Class discussion

Q3. Discuss and write down some of the ways you can injure yourself or someone else when using tools.

_____
_____
_____
_____
_____
_____

Design and Technology in Today's World: A First Look © 2018 Basil Slynko ISBN 9780648405207

AS 5

Processes

Stock materials can be altered using one of three processes: forming, separating or combining.

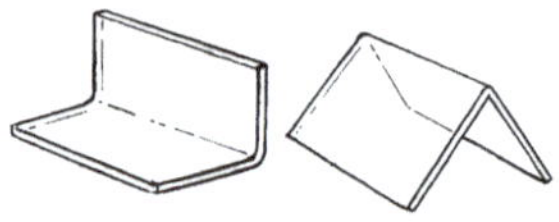

Bending

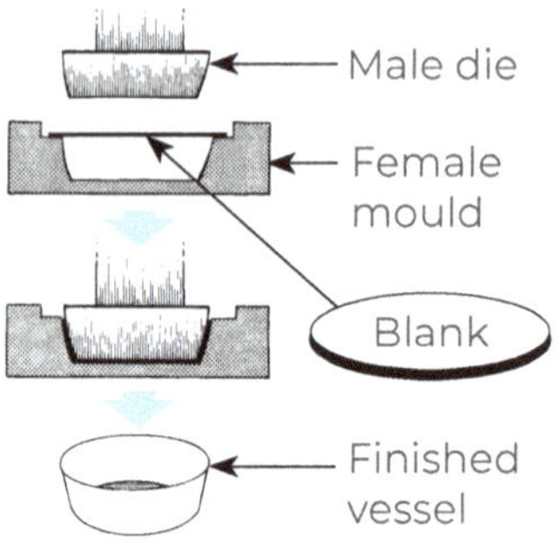
Male die
Female mould
Blank
Finished vessel

Pressing

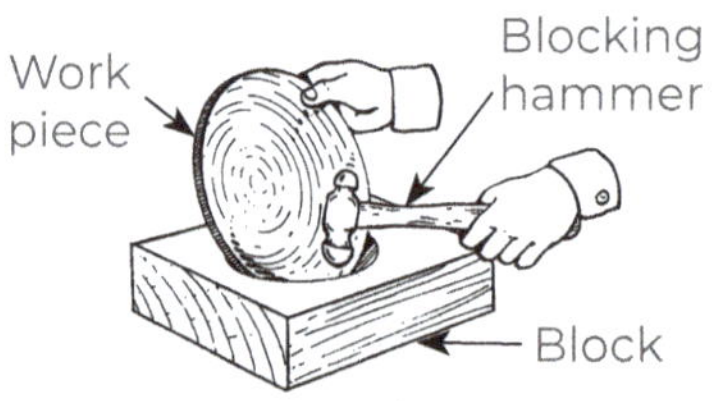
Work piece
Blocking hammer
Block

Beating

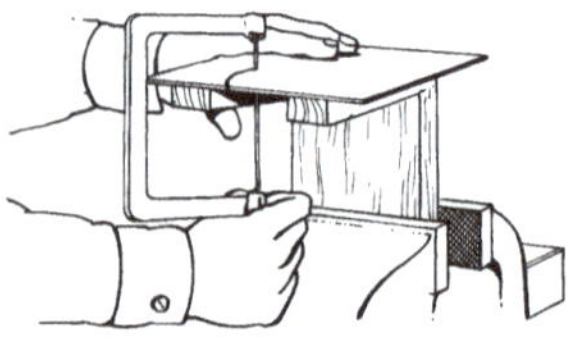

Cutting

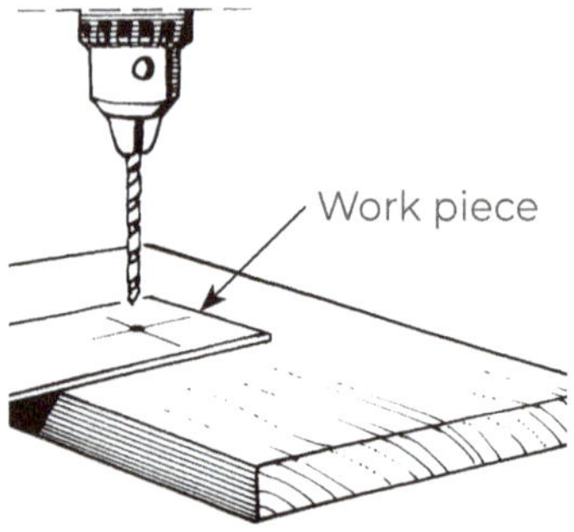
Work piece

Drilling

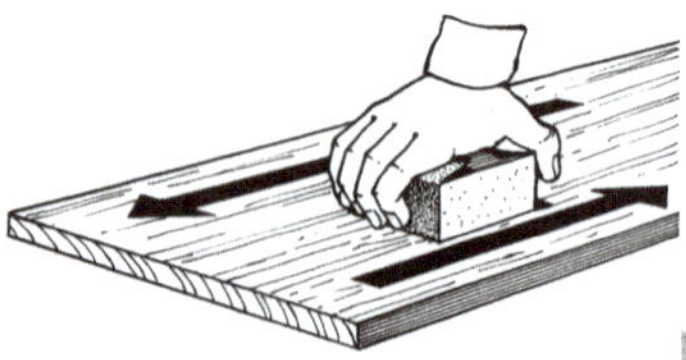

Abrading

Forming

Some common forming processes include bending, pressing and beating.

The shape of a material can be changed by **vacuum forming**.

Q1a. What is vacuum forming? Investigate and record your findings below.

____

____

____

____

____

Q1b. What materials are used in vacuum forming?

____

____

Separating

Some common separating processes include cutting, drilling and abrading.

Laser cutting is a separating process used in industry.

Q2a. Investigate and describe the laser cutting process.

____

____

____

____

____

Q2b. What are some of the advantages of using a laser?

____

____

____

____

Glues and adhesives
1. Paste – use for paper or cardboard
2. PVA glue – use for timber, paper, cardboard or fabric
3. Contact cement – use for various materials (read the instructions)
4. Hot-melt gun – a range of glue sticks is available to use with different materials
5. Tapes (sticky, duct, masking) – a quick and easy way to join many materials. Some tapes can be easily removed; for example, masking tape.

Mechanical fasteners
6. Nails
7. Screws
8. Staples
9. Self-tapping screws
10. Bolts and nuts

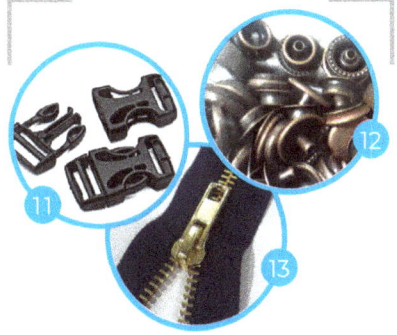

Pull-apart fasteners
11. Quick-release buckles
12. Press studs
13. Zip

Combining

Combining is the process of joining two or more materials. The joining process can be either *permanent* or *semi-permanent*. Two common products used to combine materials are glues and fasteners.

Look at the glues and fasteners on the left.

Q3. Identify three permanent combining processes and three semi-permanent combining processes. List them below.

Permanent combining processes:

1. _____

2. _____

3. _____

Semi-permanent combining processes:

1. _____

2. _____

3. _____

Class discussion

Materials can also be combined using **joints** and **cohesion**.

Q4. Discuss this as a class and then sketch some examples below.

Examples of joints:

Examples of cohesion:

What is a system?

A system is another way to create an outcome or complete a task.

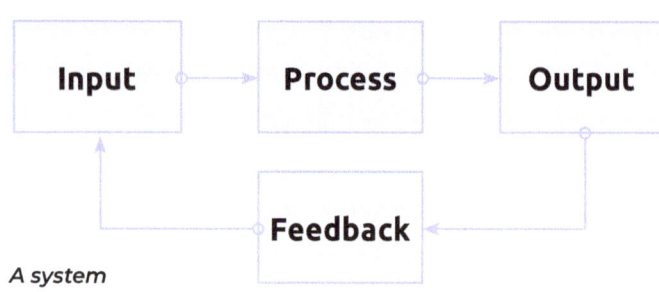

A system

An *input* is any resource that contributes to a system; for example, information, people, materials and tools.

The *process* is all the activities done to produce the result.

The *output* is the result or goal and its impacts. The impacts may be benefits or costs.

The *feedback* is the information – positive or negative – about the output. More resources may be required to improve the output.

Q1. Match each system with its outcome by filling in the table below with the outcomes from the Outcome Bank.

System	Outcome		Outcome Bank
Communication			Building structures
Transportation			Communicating with voice, text and images
Construction			Making items
Manufacturing			Moving people, animals and products

The outcome of a reverse-cycle air conditioner is to:
- cool the air
- heat the air
- control the set temperature.

Systems are usually made up of a number of sub-systems.

There are three basic sub-systems in a reverse-cycle air conditioner. The first one is the control sub-system.

Q2. What are the other two sub-systems?

Q2a. the _____ sub-system

Q2b. the _____ sub-system

Class discussion

Q3. As a class, identify and write down five other systems and their outcomes:

1. _____ Outcome: _____
2. _____ Outcome: _____
3. _____ Outcome: _____
4. _____ Outcome: _____
5. _____ Outcome: _____

Technological systems

Technological systems solve problems and produce outcomes. Let's have a look at one type of technological system: manufacturing.

1 Manufacturing systems

A **manufacturing system** enables people to make items that people want and avoid delays.

A manufacturing system

Q1. Do an internet search to find a CAD/CAM-system video clip. Choose a category such as dental, musical instruments or jewellery. Select a video to view. Then answer the questions below.

Q1a. What item is being made? _____

Q1b. What tools were used to make the item?

_____
_____
_____

Small-group activity

Q2. Discuss what you have learnt about the CAD/CAM process. Write about your discussion here.

_____
_____
_____
_____
_____
_____
_____

Class discussion

Q3a. Discuss the meaning of the term 'product life cycle'. Write its meaning here.

_____
_____
_____
_____

Q3b. Assess the positive and negative effects of the term 'product life cycle'. List them below.

Effects of a product life cycle

Positive effects	Negative effects

Small-group activity

Different products have different life cycles.

Select a product that you use every day. What is it? _____ . How long do you think this product could last? _____

Think of three ways you could reuse this product:

1. _____
2. _____
3. _____

Technological systems

Technological systems solve problems and produce outcomes. Let's have a look at another type of technological system: construction.

2 Construction systems

A **construction system** enables people to plan and build structures in an organised way and avoid delays.

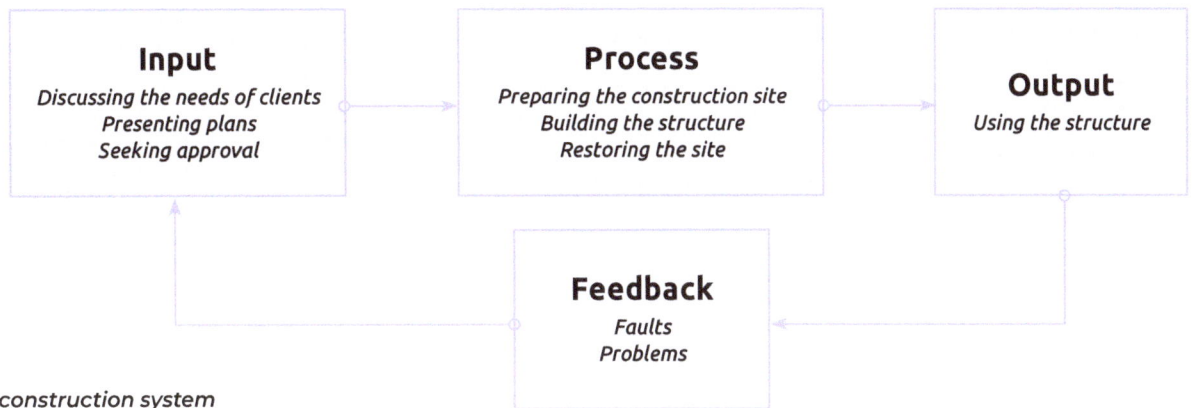

A construction system

Q1. Do an internet search to find videos of world-famous structures. Choose a structure and watch the video. Then answer the questions below.

Q1a. The structure I have chosen is _____ .

Q1b. What type of structure is it? *(Circle the correct answer.)*   Frame structure   /   Shell structure

 **Strength**
How easy or difficult is it to break?

 **Toughness**
How much impact can it stand without breaking?

 **Hardness**
How well does it resist denting or scratching?

 **Elasticity**
How well does it return to its original shape and size after being subjected to external loads and forces?

 **Density**
How heavy or light is it for its size?

 **Conductivity**
How well does it conduct or insulate against heat, electricity or sound?

 **Flammability**
How easily does it burn or smoulder when exposed to heat or fire?

 **Durability**
How well does it resist environmental stresses such as weather or insects, or does it tear easily or wear out (e.g. fabric)?

Look at the illustrations above.

Q1c. Write some of the materials used to build the structure you chose in the table on the right.

Q1d. Write the main property of each material that made it suitable to use.

Material	Main property

Q1e. List three interesting facts about the construction of this structure.

Fact 1: _____

Fact 2: _____

Fact 3: _____

Q1f. Were there any faults and/or problems with the construction of the structure? Describe some of the faults and/or problems below.

_____
_____
_____
_____
_____
_____

Small-group activity

Q2. The planning stage of construction looks at the needs of the client. Imagine your client wants to build a private hospital. Analyse the needs of a hospital and record them below.

_____
_____
_____
_____
_____
_____

Class discussion

Q3. Record any other needs of a hospital that your group did not identify.

_____
_____
_____
_____
_____

Agricultural systems

Agricultural systems enable people to produce food and fibre in an organised way.

Input
Soil
Seeds
Animals
Water

Process
Planting and/or breeding
Fertilising and/or feeding
Harvesting
Selling

Output
Food produce and/or animals
Fibre
Waste

Feedback
Quantity
Quality
Wastage
Impacts on the environment

An agricultural system

Do an internet search to find a video of an agricultural system. Then answer the questions below.

Q1a. What type of agricultural system is it? Use the Word Bank to select your answer.

It is a(n) _____ agricultural system.

Word Bank
mixed-farm
extensive
intensive

Q1b. What is the produce: food and/or fibre? _____

Q1c. List some of the sub-systems.

_____
_____
_____
_____

Q1d. Write down three interesting facts about this agricultural system.

Fact 1: _____
_____
_____

Fact 2: _____
_____
_____

Fact 3: _____
_____
_____

Small-group activity

Q2. Investigate some of the practices used to maintain food safety and hygiene of produce such as apples, potatoes, strawberries and eggs – from paddock to shelf.

Select a produce and list the purpose of each practice in the table below. The first practice has been completed as a guide.

The produce I have selected is _____.

Practice	Purpose
Washing	To remove dirt and to clean the produce
Drying	
Inspection	
Packaging	

Class discussion

Q3. All fresh produce has a shelf life. It could be a couple of days or several weeks. Investigate some of the ways used to extend the shelf life of produce. Write some of your findings below.

_____
_____
_____
_____
_____

Control systems

A **control system** completes a task in an organised way.

There are two kinds of control systems:
- open-loop
- closed-loop.

 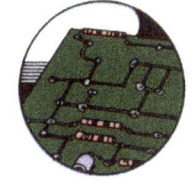 

Input　　　　　Process　　　　　Output

An **open-loop control system** has no way of checking its output because there is no feedback.

An open-loop control system

A **closed-loop control system** has a way of checking its output. It can monitor/check the output because of feedback. The system can stop the output once the action is done.

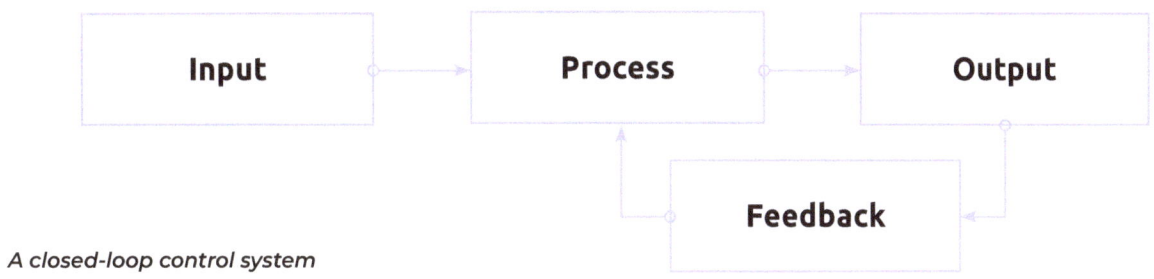

A closed-loop control system

Q1. Tick the correct type of control system for each item below.

Refrigerator
☐ Open-loop
☐ Closed-loop

Toilet cistern
☐ Open-loop
☐ Closed-loop

Sprinkler
☐ Open-loop
☐ Closed-loop

Class discussion

Q2. Think of another five items with control systems. Write them in the table below. Then identify the type of control system for each item.

Item	Type of control system
1.	- loop system
2.	- loop system
3.	- loop system
4.	- loop system
5.	- loop system

Technology and the future

Technology and the future has always been an issue for people. Back in the 1980s, people were concerned about the costs of technology. A new acronym was introduced: **NIMBY**.

Q1. What does NIMBY stand for?

N __ __   I __   M __   B __ __ __   Y __ __ __

Q2. What is the meaning of NIMBY?

_____
_____
_____
_____

Q3. Use the internet to identify a recycling activity in your community. Answer the questions below.

Q3a. What waste is recycled? _____

Q3b. How is this waste recycled? _____
_____
_____
_____
_____

Small-group activity

Q4a. Think: What other waste in your community could be recycled?

_____
_____
_____
_____

Q4b. How could this waste be recycled? Record your ideas below.

_____
_____
_____
_____

New technologies are being developed to meet the needs of society. What technologies would you like to use in the future? Think of three technologies and complete the activities below.

Q5a. Use the space below to present a design of your first technology.
Add notes to describe any features that you cannot sketch.

My first technology is _____.

Notes:

_____

_____

_____

Evaluate the costs and benefits of this technology.

Costs	Benefits

Q5b. Use the space below to present a design of your second technology.
Add notes to describe any features that you cannot sketch.

My second technology is _____ .

Notes:

_____

_____

_____

Evaluate the costs and benefits of this technology.

Costs	Benefits

Q5c. Use the space below to present a design of your third technology.
Add notes to describe any features that you cannot sketch.

My third technology is _____ .

Notes:
_____
_____
_____

Evaluate the costs and benefits of this technology.

Costs	Benefits

Class discussion

Q6. Share one of your technologies presented in Question 5 with your classmates.
Record the feedback – both positive and negative – in the table below.

The technology I shared is _____.

Positive comments	Negative comments

Q7. In the space below, present a new design of your technology to reflect the feedback from your class. Add notes to describe features that you cannot sketch.

Notes:
_____
_____

Q8. Now assess the value of your technology presented in Question 6.
_____
_____
_____

Safety

Safety is necessary to stop something bad from happening to you. Remember that accidents can happen anywhere, any time.

Safety posters

Select one of the safety posters shown above. The poster I chose is number _____.

Q1a. What is the safety message in the poster you chose?

Message:_____

_____

_____

_____

_____

Q1b. Is it easy to understand?   Yes ☐   No ☐

Why/why not?_____

_____

_____

_____

_____

Do an internet search for 'safety posters'. You should find that the safety posters are presented in categories; for example: workplace safety posters, posters for children's safety, industrial safety posters and health safety posters.

Q2. Select one safety poster from each of three categories. Sketch the safety posters below. Give each safety poster a title and explain why you like it.

My title for this poster is _____ .

I like this poster because _____
_____
_____
_____
_____
_____
_____
_____ .

My title for this poster is _____ .

I like this poster because _____
_____
_____
_____
_____
_____
_____
_____ .

My title for this poster is _____ .

I like this poster because _____
_____
_____
_____
_____
_____
_____
_____ .

Small-group activity

Q3. Share your safety poster images and explain why you like them.
Write any feedback below.

Safety poster 1: _____
_____

Safety poster 2: _____
_____

Safety poster 3: _____
_____

Personal Protective Equipment (PPE) is the general term used to describe safety gear.

Q4. Write down an outdoor activity of your choice.

My activity is _____.

In the table below, indicate what PPE is needed to protect a body part(s) when doing this activity.

What body part(s) need to be protected?	PPE to be worn

Congratulations!

You have finished all the activities.

You should now be able to complete the last column of the KWL chart at the front of the book.

After finishing the KWL Chart, visit **www.professorbaz.com.au** to print your Certificate of Achievement.

Notes:

Notes:

Notes:

Notes:

Notes:

Find-a-word solution:

```
E X T S N O I T A R E D I S N O C Q A J W E M H C
L N H F A V S U S T A I N A B I L I T Y V A A H K
E D O G Y C O L L O B O R A T I O N H H L D T N A
C R U N E G N I D L I U B P O L E V E D J B E E G
T O G I X R T U P T U O W P M M C E F U T U R E R
R B H N P R E P A R A T I O N O I S S U C S I D I
I O T R A Z E C L C O M P O N E N T S F R N A S C
C T S A N T I S A A P D R L Q J I I E L D N L B U
I I D E S F U J O A C I U H U N R G T U O K S E L
T C F L I L P R C U V I T C G S H A S O R O G E T
Y S K C O T V T A N R G N I T S E T A O R K T M U
M G E I N R I U E L O C S H Q I R I W I H I E K R
J P R T N H T V O A R I E T C Y O O I O S S N M E
S O H E T P G N I D N A T S R E D N U O U O F G E
I L E H N E U W O T H E C A M U T T P A W L W C X
N L S T E E C T E C C S G O R E C M C L H U O H T
T U U N M V W H S H H A D A N O O T E P C T R A E
E T O Y P S R A N O A E B S M C L D U J R I L N N
G I H S I E U I B O L I I E V S G P P R A O D G S
R O N M U Q Q U Z L L V S A F E T Y X H E N I E I
A N E E Q U S Q I J E O I K N P R O C E S S E S V
T T E T E E X N T A N O G N I N N A L P E O P L E
I A R S S N G Y N T G R K Y G L R B C D R X G A P
O U G Y K C A B D E E F F E C T L I T E N S I O N
N T A S A E D I K D M E C H A N I S A T I O N G X
```

www.ingramcontent.com/pod-product-compliance
Lightning Source LLC
Chambersburg PA
CBHW061536010526
44107CB00066B/2885